Tell Me Why

WHY?

I Throw Up

Katie Marsico

Published in the United States of America by Cherry Lake Publishing
Ann Arbor, Michigan
www.cherrylakepublishing.com

Content Adviser: Charisse Gencyuz, M.D., Clinical Instructor, Department of Internal Medicine, University of Michigan
Reading Adviser: Marla Conn, ReadAbility, Inc.

Photo Credits: © bonzodog/Shutterstock Images, cover, 1, 15; © Samuel Borges Photography/ Shutterstock Images, cover, 1, 11; © rmnoa357/Shutterstock Images, cover, 1, 21; © ron sumners/ Thinkstock, cover, 1, 13; © Fuse/Thinkstock, cover, 1, 5; © Sebastian Kaulitzki/Thinkstock, cover, 1, 7; © michaeljung/Shutterstock Images, back cover; © MSPhotographic/Shutterstock Images, 9; © Alena Hovorkova/Shutterstock Images, 11; © mubus7/Shutterstock Images, 15; © vgajic/iStock, 17; © wavebreakmedia/Shutterstock Images, 19; © Jaimie Duplass/Shutterstock Images, 21

Library of Congress Cataloging-in-Publication Data

Marsico, Katie, 1980- author.
  I throw up / by Katie Marsico.
     pages cm. -- (Tell me why)
  Summary: "Offers answers to the most compelling questions about rumbling tummies. Age-appropriate explanations and appealing photos. Additional text features and search tools, including a glossary and an index, help students locate information and learn new words."-- Provided by publisher.
  Audience: K to grade 3.
  Includes bibliographical references and index.
  ISBN 978-1-63188-006-3 (hardcover) -- ISBN 978-1-63188-049-0 (pbk.) -- ISBN 978-1-63188-092-6 (pdf) -- ISBN 978-1-63188-135-0 (ebook) 1. Digestion--Juvenile literature--Miscellanea. 2. Digestive organs--Juvenile literature--Miscellanea. 3. Vomiting--Juvenile literature--Miscellanea. 4. Gastroenteritis--Juvenile literature--Miscellanea. 5. Children's questions and answers. I. Title.

QP145.M368 2015
612.3--dc23
                              2014005671

Cherry Lake Publishing would like to acknowledge the work of The Partnership for 21st Century Skills. Please visit www.p21.org for more information.

Printed in the United States of America
Corporate Graphics Inc.

Table of Contents

Tummy Troubles

No school for Ming today! He is staying home, but he won't be doing anything fun. His belly is aching, and his throat is dry. After breakfast, he began throwing up.

Throwing up, or vomiting, is something the body doesn't have control over. When a person throws up, the contents of the stomach are forced up the **esophagus** and out the mouth.

It's normal to feel sick if you throw up.

Vomit usually contains bits of food and stomach acid. It's also often made up of saliva, or spit. Sometimes **bile** and blood are found in vomit as well.

There are many reasons people throw up. **Germs** and **parasites** are often to blame. These are tiny living organisms. Sometimes germs and parasites cause infections, or illnesses. They trigger vomiting by **irritating** body parts involved in **digestion**.

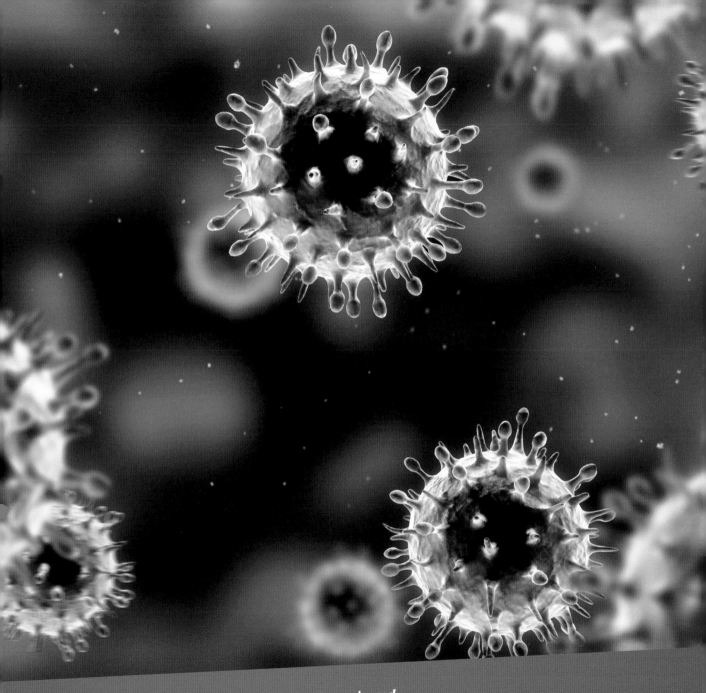

This is what a flu virus looks like when viewed under a microscope.

Not a Normal Breakfast

Most days, Ming has a healthy breakfast. Yet this morning, he isn't even able to keep down dry toast! Every time he tries eating, he throws up.

Normally Ming's digestive system is busy breaking down food into **nutrients**. It also turns whatever food the body doesn't use into waste products.

You may not be able to eat your usual breakfast if you've been throwing up.

Liver

The digestive system starts at the mouth and esophagus. People chew and swallow food. Then it passes into the stomach and through tube-shaped **organs** called intestines. Along the way, acids and other chemicals change food into nutrients and waste. The intestines absorb, or take in, nutrients. Meanwhile, the body releases solid waste through an opening called the anus.

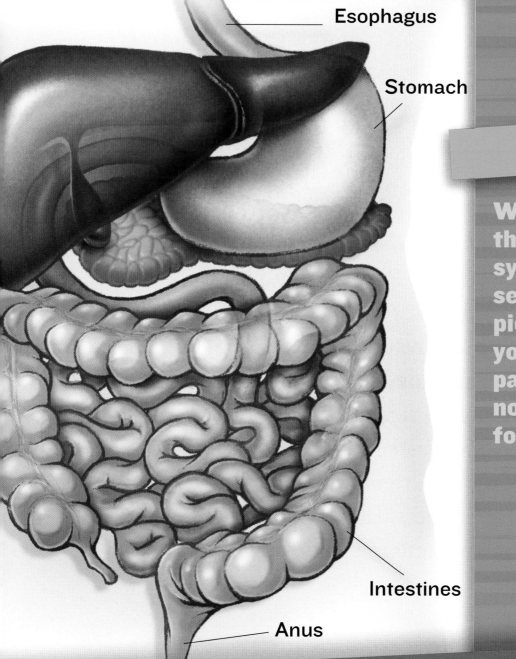

Esophagus

Stomach

Intestines

Anus

LOOK!

What parts of the digestive system do you see in this picture? Can you trace the path that food normally follows?

Did you know this is what the inside of your body looks like?

Upside-Down Digestion

Ming tries telling himself he's not going to vomit. But it doesn't work. He still keeps racing to the bathroom!

Ming's mom says he probably has gastroenteritis. This condition occurs when a person's digestive system is irritated. Germs and parasites both cause gastroenteritis. Ming is shocked that tiny organisms can make such a huge mess! How do they turn his entire digestive system upside down?

You can't always control when you're going to throw up.

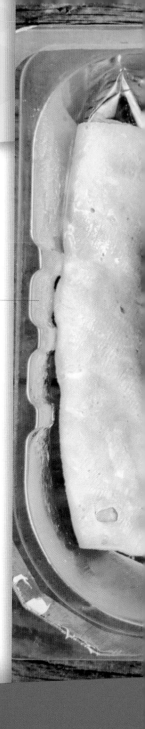

Gastroenteritis triggers the body to send a chemical message to the brain. It lets the brain know that something is bothering the digestive system. The brain responds by sending signals back to body parts involved in digestion.

What else besides gastroenteritis could make a person throw up?

This meat has turned green because it hasn't been stored properly. Eating it could make you sick!

This sets the digestive system in motion. It begins to contract, or tighten. By contracting and relaxing, the stomach and intestines force their contents up the esophagus. They finally leave the mouth as vomit.

Gastroenteritis can be painful.

Finally Feeling Better

By dinner, Ming no longer feels nauseous, or sick to his stomach. He sips clear chicken **broth**. It stays down! Ming's mom explains that his digestive system was irritated. So it will take time before it can begin doing its job normally again.

Gastroenteritis usually lasts a few days to a week. It often causes nausea and **diarrhea**. Bad cases of gastroenteritis lead to dehydration.

You'll get better quicker if you now how to treat gastroenteritis.

Dehydration is when the body loses more **fluid** than it absorbs. Some signs of dehydration are dry mouth, dizziness, and headache. Ming doesn't want to get dehydrated.

Ming eats ice chips, frozen fruit bars, clear broth, and crackers for the next 24 hours. A day later, he's back to his old self . . . and his normal breakfast!

MAKE A GUESS!

Can you guess other reasons why someone would become dehydrated?

Drinking fluids will help you avoid dehydration.

21

Think About It

What if people were not able to throw up? Do you think this would be good or bad for their health? Can you think of a benefit to throwing up?

Go online with an adult or visit your library. Find photos of germs and parasites. Compare the differences between the two. Are there any similarities?

Do you think hand-washing is a way to prevent gastroenteritis from spreading to others? Why or why not?

Glossary

bile (BYLE) a brownish-green fluid that helps the body digest food

broth (BRAWTH) a liquid food mixture often used in soup

diarrhea (dye-uh-REE-uh) a condition in which the digestive system produces waste that is more liquid than solid

digestion (dye-JESS-chuhn) the process the body uses to break down food into nutrients and waste

esophagus (ih-SOF-uh-guss) a stretchy passage that connects the mouth with the stomach

fluid (FLOO-uhd) a substance such as water that has no fixed shape and that flows easily

germs (JUHRMZ) tiny organisms that often produce disease

irritating (IR-uh-tayt-ing) producing discomfort or pain

nutrients (NU-tree-uhntz) substances that living things need to grow and stay healthy

organs (OR-guhnz) body parts such as the intestines that perform a specific job

parasites (PER-uh-sytes) organisms that must live in or on another organism to survive and that often cause disease

Find Out More

Books:

Halvorson, Karin, and Diane Craig (consulting editor). *Inside the Stomach*. Minneapolis: ABDO Publishing Co., 2013.

Johnson, Rebecca L. *Your Digestive System*. Minneapolis: Lerner Publications Co., 2013.

Lew, Kristi. *Farts, Vomit, and Other Functions That Help Your Body*. Mankato, MN: Capstone Press, 2011.

Web Sites:

Discovery Kids—Your Digestive System
www.kids.discovery.com/tell-me/science/body-systems/your-digestive-system
Get a closer look at how the human body digests food.

KidsHealth—What's Puke?
www.kidshealth.org/kid/talk/yucky/puke.html
Read more about the physical processes involved in vomiting.

Index

About the Author

Katie Marsico is the author of more than 150 children's books. She lives in a suburb of Chicago, Illinois, with her husband and children.